DOOR 2

CREATING OPPORTUNITIES

KASY SPEARS

FAWKES PUBLISHING, LLC

DOOR 2

CREATING OPPORTUNITIES

Author: Kasy Spears
Social Media: @Simplykasy @kasyspears
YouTube, Twitter, podcasts, and Linkedin
Published By: Fawkes Publishing, LLC Copyright © 2018 . All Rights Reserved.
Orginally Published
ISBN-13: 978-1727303407
ISBN-10: 1727303407

Cover Design: Kasondra Spears
Literary Agent: Selina Page
Edited by : John Hunt

Fawkes Publishing , LLC

First Edition

Printed in
Austin Texas USA

DEDICATION

To my Mom Kathryn, Father Mark,
Brother Josh.

In memory of my Grandparents and my fur
babies.

To my two dogs Duke and Prince.

Kasy Spears

CONTENTS

CONTENTS

CONTENTS

About the Author

Kasy is an International Best-Selling Author, Motivational Coach and Business Strategist. I was born in the north and grew up in the south. I have traveled to many locations some as a solo traveler. I have written many books some flops and some still my best sellers. I have a unique sense of humor or maybe it's not so unique? I am a giant nerd and I like to learn and love technology. Hold on maybe love hate technology. I have to disconnect from my cyber world to appreciate the little things like birds singing with no noise around. I am a very very nice person and very helpful. I have been bullied a lot and it sucks donkey. I married a psycho who still stalks me and yes, it is so messed up I wrote a book about it and yes that is an international best seller. I would like to convert it to a script and maybe make it a movie it's that twisted ya'll. I am a photographer and video person. I love movies and random things. I am in a category of my own.

I have my own unique cuss words that make people laugh "fudge monkey" it makes me think of those bananas dipped in fudge and I am not a banana person and then it makes me think of a cartoon monkey dripping in fudge. I say oh Mylanta (thanks Full House). let's face it; am I weird? Well I do live in Austin

Texas and the city is known for Keep Austin Weird. I am going to share with you things that work for me.

That is me in a nutshell but I really can't fit in a nutshell…

I am about to be change your world. What you are about to learn can be applied in any business, and in your personal life. A little about me I am a Texas Real Estate Broker who had no sphere of influence and have been in real estate full time since 2007 with no sphere of influence. Most would tell you without a sphere you will fail. For the most part that is very true my journey has not been easy. Most Brokers keep their tools of the trade a secrete so learning was a series of mistakes and learning and trying new ways. I have spent a ton of money that if I had known what I know now I could have saved that money. I have lived off my credit cards I have been broke, let me say BROKE! I have been abused by my husband who is a bigamist in a church in norther California . I have been harassed n hunted by his women. Trust me I wrote a book on it. It is the stuff of movies but I am living it. I have been to Hell and back and yes I actually drove and have a t shirt from Hell. If I can make it in real estate and business with all my obstacles you can too!

No matter where you are there are three types of people:

1. You have time and no money.

2. You have money and no time.

3. You have time and money but have no idea how to start

When you have no money, your road is going to be longer and more challenging but yes you can do it. You invest in sweat, tears and years in your idea. The second one is you have money but you do not have the time. You will then have to trade off what is important for much needed time in your idea may be less tv, or time with family friends ... These people surprisingly are the hardest to get their idea off the ground. They are so used to the stability of a steady check that taking a risk is very scary for them. These people want their ducks in a row. That is an illusion you will never have your ducks in a row life gets in the way every time.

The last one is you have both time and money but you have no clue how to bridge the gap of your idea and getting it launched off the ground. Oh, people will have their hands out to you with every promise under the sun and no delivery at this point you will need to be wise with your money and the people in your circle.

Regardless you can be successful as BIG business you just have to learn how to build a door.

It is truly possible to live your dream and see your ideas come to life. However, everything has a cost. As in the show Once Upon a Time "All *magic comes with a price".* I have coached actors on how to use this formula to get acting gigs. I have shown companies small and large how to up their game. I have written books, spoken at conferences, tv radio show and yes you too can be a part of this group. I must warn you there are predators in the waters and yes you will be swimming with sharks just know this people will try and convince you to buy their solutions, they will steal your idea and then they will try and say terrible things about you to remove you from there pond. Just don't loss who you are your humanity in the process. Let them steal your ideas. If a person is so low to steal and idea then let them. I really did say that. If a person is willing to do whatever it takes and hurt whom ever to rise to the top. You cannot stop bad things from happening . What you do is build a support door. You move on to your next idea. The person who steals ideas will not have and new fresh ideas they will be on old ones. Let them chase you. You will stand out while the thief hits the heads of all the people they hurt on the way up on their way down. You can only rise so far with secrets in your closet eventually the door pops open. It's the sand castle effect the tide always washes it away.

Think   of   this   you're

in a room with no door, no windows and on the other side is your success. How long will you be in this room is dependent on you. You have no tools and you know you need clients but they are outside and you are inside.

How do you reach them?

You need to build a door.

How do I build a door with no tools?

Simply you invent them.

Ok how do I invent tools with nothing?

Good question.

Stop looking at what you do not have and start thinking about what you do have. You have pants on use buttons to create a carving tool. Use your muscles to carve at the weak spots on the wall, floor and keep carving at the weak spots until a hole emerges and then from their make a bigger opening and soon you will have a door. Each person has a different room and different items in a room some have nothing but an idea. How badly do you want your idea? How much are you willing to work for it. Sometimes even for free. I had no tools and I had to work for free to get the word out and to gather examples of my work to build a door to paid opportunities. If you read my book series based on my life married to a psychotic, narcissistic sociopath you will understand just how little I had and the Hell I had to crawl out of to build my door. You will always be building doors to travel thru it never ends.

You need to understand the basic when you understand the basics you can start to build your first door.

Teaching:

Teaching is repeating until learning takes place.

Learning:

Learning is hearing and doing until understanding takes place. Also learning is hearing over and over again until understanding takes place.

To realizing your dream of being a VET, Husband, Wife, Parent, Step Parent, Real Estate Broker, Actor, Model, Business Owner…. You MUST rinse and repeat the process over and over again. If you went to one casting call and that was it you will never realize your dream. If you tried out one time for the team you will always be on the bench.

You must do things over and over again until the understanding takes place. You might not get it the first time, the second time, you might not even get it the fifth time but by doing it over and over again until the understanding takes place. Sometimes we need to hear the same things over and over again until understanding kicks in, and this applies to children as well, how many times have we had to repeat yourself until the learning kicks in.

Attitude has a lot to play into with your success. You will without a doubt have people put you down make fun of you for your dream. You may even have your own family tell you to quit your dream because you have other priorities that come first, or simple just because they cannot see it they will tell you to go traditional routes have your ducks in a row. Reality is no one ever has their ducks in a row life gets in the way. That is simply a road block you set up for not pursuing your dream. Let look a people who were told you can't, you won't make it, it simple is not for you. These people are no more special than you. What separates them from us is they kept making doors until one clicked.

FAMOUS FAILURES GRID

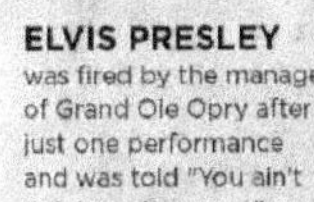

ELVIS PRESLEY
was fired by the manager of Grand Ole Opry after just one performance and was told "You ain't goin' nowhere son."

FAMOUS FAILURE SERIES

IF YOU'VE NEVER FAILED
YOU'VE NEVER TRIED ANYTHING NEW

BEETHOVEN'S
teachers felt he was hopeless at composing and that he would never succeed with the violin.

FAMOUS FAILURE SERIES

IF YOU'VE NEVER FAILED
YOU'VE NEVER TRIED ANYTHING NEW

In his first screen test,
FRED ASTAIRE
was told he can't act, can't sing, was slightly bald, but can dance a little. He went on to become an incredibly successful actor, singer and dancer.

FAMOUS FAILURE SERIES

IF YOU'VE NEVER FAILED
YOU'VE NEVER TRIED ANYTHING NEW

THE BEATLES
were told by a recording company that they didn't like their sound and that guitar music was on the way out.

FAMOUS FAILURE SERIES

IF YOU'VE NEVER FAILED
YOU'VE NEVER TRIED ANYTHING NEW

ALBERT EINSTEIN
wasn't able to speak until he was four and didn't read until he was seven, causing his teachers and parents to think he was mentally handicapped, slow and anti-social.

FAMOUS FAILURE SERIES

IF YOU'VE NEVER FAILED
YOU'VE NEVER TRIED ANYTHING NEW

AKIO MORITA'S first product, a rice cooker, sold less than 100 units. This first setback didn't stop him as he pushed forward to create the multi-billion dollar company, Sony.

FAMOUS FAILURE SERIES

IF YOU'VE NEVER FAILED
YOU'VE NEVER TRIED ANYTHING NEW

Welcome to the club, Be the loser, the weirdo and just keep trying. Most people are three doors away from pay dirt when they finally give up. Just take one more step.

One thing that will cause you to lose your battle to get your idea or dream into reality is tools. Actors this is researching plays, movies and taking classes, headshots, extra work learning the craft and rehearsing it.

Models it is also researching and learning the craft. Real Estate people

and another business learn your craft, do your homework!

Door 1

Knowledge

The first thing you have to do is know your product. When you guys don't know your products or services you kill your brand. Don't talk about products you don't know about you hurt yourself and you hurt the company the other thing you have to know is know your limitations what is the max amount of people you can service with your product. Many business owners say I do everything. I want all the customers I can get. You are dead wrong in this thinking. What you really need to know is the maximum amount of customers that you can handle with your product or service because this will help you determine the scale and the scope of your marketing campaign. If you are a small business owner with a limited budget then no you can't service everyone and do everything it is impossible. Jack of all trades expert in none. You just killed your business and your brand. You have to know your target market. You need to know your demographics where are your clients that you need for your products and services. Here is how you create leads based on your target clients based upon that.

Example:

What is the job of a wide receiver in football?

Most would think the job of the wide receiver is to catch the ball.

I disagree with this logic. The job of the wide receiver is not to catch the ball. Now let think of this logically. If you are a professional player it is assumed the least you can do is to catch a ball. Now all wide receivers catch balls, that is their job. However that is not their job. The job of a wide receiver **is to separate from the competition** . Think about it if a wide receiver cannot separate from the competition they will never be able to get a touchdown. Your team will never win the game. All because the wide receiver cannot separate from the competition.

I will ask you this what is your job as a professional?

Lawyers your job is to defend our client vigorously. Maybe you're an Actor, Model, Real Estate agent or even a sales person. A sales persons job is not to sell as much product as they can. No your job in any profession is simply.

to separate from the competition.

There are millions of people with real estate license in the country all real estate agents can sell houses because they have their license to do so. However their job is not to sell houses it is to separate from the competition. **The closer you are to the competition the harder it is for you to catch a client.** What do I mean by being too close to the competition.

Look at your business card.

Does it look like their business cards?

Your website does it look like their website?

You're following the competition. You have two choices in business you can be leading the comp. or you can be following it.

Which are you?

To separate from your comp., you HAVE to know your products and services. What I mean is you focus on one product or service.

Example:

Real estate agents can sell land, property manage, commercial, buyers, sellers, farm, mobile homes, tiny homes...

Military, divorce, last will or probate, moving, up sizing, downsizing, nursing home bound... North of your city, central, south, east west

Luxury, mid-price, low price, foreclosure, short sales, reo, 1031, HUD.... Endless client base.

Who is your target audience?

How do you reach them?

who are they?

Today when you're working on your business don't be the serial entrepreneurs anyone can do that. Today focus on one business, one product. Don't start on another product or services until you've maxed out your first business product or service. Don't start till the first is automated or can run without you in charge.

Know your limitations.

What is the maximum amount of people you can service with your product?

You have to know this because this will determine the scope and scale of your marketing campaign. When you go online believe me you can meet as many people as you want. However, if you cannot service them all, you're going to kill your brand immediately. Because good marketing is knowing who you're talking to. Marketing is not about being politically correct. Marketing is about being correct.

You've got to know your target market. Stop spinning your wheels running behind clients. That will never do business with you. That ends today. This is a hard task for most business owners. Switch your thinking.

You need to know what clients you want and which clients you want to

keep out.

Which customers waste your time?

Which customers waste valuable resources?

Which customers you don't want to do business with?

Know Your Comp.

As a business owner you have got to know your competition. Remember

your job as a professional is not to just use your job to sell houses to sell

workouts or to sell whatever product or service you sell .... **your job is**

to separate yourself from the competition.

> *"The closer you are to the competition the harder it is for you to*
>
> *catch a client".*

What are three things I can do to separate myself from the competition?

1. Know your competition inside and out. A lot of times you can look at what they're doing and do it better. I can take it I can rename it repurpose it and reuse it and make money!

Door 2

Efficiency

In business you have to be efficient. One thing that is true about entrepreneurs is the fact that they believe that they can do it all. The problem with entrepreneurs, is that they actually believe that. You're not Super Human! If you truly want to leap tall buildings with a single bound you have to have a plan of action in order to do it.

What is the number one problem with entrepreneurs?

Every day I am hustling….

I've got to make some money.

I have bills to pay.

Most entrepreneurs are in a rush from the 21st through the first every month. I want you to know business is not a race, it is a process.

Race

A race is defined by who finishes first.

In the process of winning in business is defined by finishing.

Finishing

Finishing is defined by anything done to the point where it can go on without you being in the process. Anything that can go on without your on-site supervision. If you cannot walk away from your business. It is not finished.

To be a successful in business you need to set up process or plans of action. The first thing you need is a business plan and inside your business plan should be your marketing plan, followed by your action plan and your strategic plan.

The order in which you should have these plans are:

1. Business Plan

2. Strategic Plan

3. Marketing Plan

4. Action Plan

Why do most business not have these plans of action? One big reason is it was confusing and too dang hard to create.

I have a rule and here's the rule I believe that if the work is too hard you got the wrong to tool. One of the things we do in business is we make it way too hard. Today I want to simplify your lives. It is one of my popular saying and when I think of a challenging situation I think of this guy. MacGyver. What I want you guys to do is to become the MacGyver's in your business and life.

"If the works too hard you got the wrong tools"

Here are some very helpful tools to help you in your business:

Business plan TOOLS:

Get yourself a **FREE** business plan

enloop.com

Strategic plan you can go to **profitably.com** they walk you through it step

by step just answer the questions.

How many customers would you like to attract?

What day did you start your business.?

They spit out your business plan you can have a business plan in under

one hour FREE!

Door 3

Engagement

How are you engaging your clients?

What tools are you using to engage your clients?

Social media is the dominant force in business today. If your business does not use social media effectively then you will be like Toys R Us, Blockbuster, Radio Shack… Many of us are not using social media correctly. We are not using social media in a way that will constantly engage our clients.

Once reason it's confusing there is a lot of platforms to choose from and the other is time. I want you guys to make a note: there are only so many things you can do for free however you do need to invest in your business financially with tools as well. Every three months without fail I buy a new tool for my business every month. I make a list of new tools and for every year I have a list of tools I want to buy every month. When

I generate a certain amount of revenue I go out and buy the tool and I know exactly which ones I want. This is key to being ahead of your competitors.

I have a course called Pixel Pickle be a social media Unicorn. Navigating the confusing world of social media. How to maximizing your social media for business. In this course I am going to give you knowledge and tools to use in your business.

Also, when you think about engaging your clients think of a man on one  knee proposing. This signifies an approach from humility. Not only is he on one knee but he also has a ring in his hand the ring represents incentivizing the process. Not only should you be thinking about approaching your client from a position of humility. Also, how are you going to incentivizing the process. What am I talking about in incentivizing the process. I'm not talking about paying your customers.

I'm talking about what the benefits of somebody being your client?

What are the benefits of the benefits. I want you to think deeper about your clients. Now going back to the guy on one knee he could be saying:

"hey I have a big house and a fast car I have all this money...."

No what he should be saying is:

"I will respect you, I will appreciate you.... I come from a family whose values your intelligence."

When you're talking about your products and services with your clients sometimes you're talking about what you want them to know.

I'll use this as an example:

In real estate you could talk to your client about, when you buy a home you have pride of ownership. That is old news. You should say that you will treat them with respect...

What are the benefits of working with you?

Don't talk to them about your products or services. Until you have established trust in you and your business. This is key if you wish to sell anything. If you do not establish trust you will not sell anything.

"WIIFM" = what is in it for me!

Benefits sells and products tell.

Talk to them about the difference between working with you and how you are different. Don't talk to them about the products and services the products and services generally will sell themselves. The last thing you have to do is ask. We assume people know this. We assume they know that we want to do business with them. Sometimes they don't know! Make sure you ask for the business, and when you get it right there are wonderful things that happen.

Door 4

Color

Have you ever considered the significance of color in branding? **Color** plays a vast role in memory recall. It excites all the senses, instantly conveying a message like no other communication technique. Selecting the right dominant color for your brand is important. This color ought to appear on all your promotional material. You can wear your color to attract attention. Following is the most common impression each color conveys:

Blue: Cool blue is sensed as trustworthy, dependable, fiscally responsible and secure. Blue is a particularly popular color with financial institutions.

Red: Red sparks off your pituitary gland, increasing your pulse rate and causing you to breathe more rapidly. Count on red to arouse a passionate response.

Green: at large, green connotes health, freshness and serenity. Deeper greens are affiliated with wealth or prestige, while light greens are calming.

Yellow: In every society, yellow is affiliated with the sun. It communicates optimism, light and warmth. Particular shades seem to motivate and stimulate originative thought and energy. The eye sees bright yellows before any other color, making them good for point-of-purchase displays.

Purple: Purple is a color favored by originative types. It evokes mystery, sophistication, spirituality and royalty. Lavender evokes nostalgia and sentimentality.

Pink: Hot pinks express energy, youthfulness, fun and excitement. Dusty pinks seem sentimental. Lighter pinks are more romantic.

Orange: Cheerful orange arouses exuberance, fun and vitality. Orange is deemed gregarious and frequently childlike. Lighter shades appeal to an upscale market. Peach tones work well with health care, restaurants and beauty salons.

Brown: This earthy color transmits simplicity, durability and stability. Particular shades of brown, like terracotta, might convey an upscale look.

Black: Black is sober, bold, powerful and classic. It produces drama and connotes sophistication. Black works well for expensive products, but might also make a product look heavy.

White: White implies simplicity, cleanliness and purity. The human eye views white as a brilliant color, so it at once catches the eye in signage. White is frequently used with infant and health-related products.

Actors use this to your advantage in your resume, n your clothing selection and more. Find a color pallet and stick to it. You can use teal blue which is lux and peaceful and is in the blue green family. Think Tiffany's. This logo is a color and black or white simple font and boy do we love this color it is everywhere now.

COLOUR PSYCHOLOGY IN LOGO DESIGN

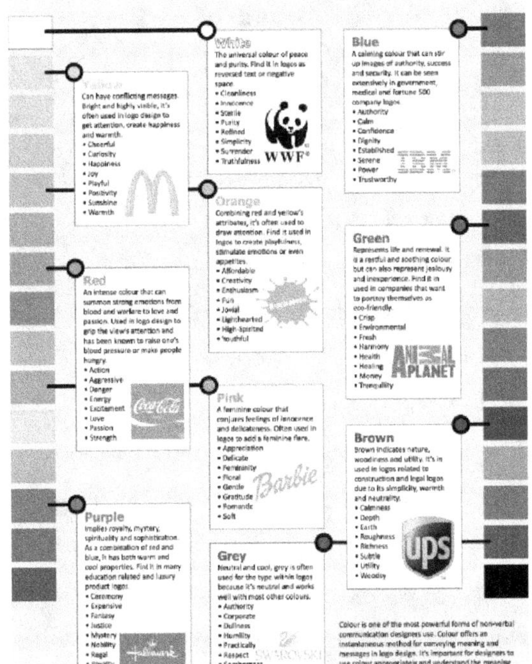

Yellow

Can have conflicting messages. Bright and highly visible, it's often used in logo design to get attention, create happiness and warmth.

- Cheerful
- Curiosity
- Happiness
- Joy
- Playful
- Positivity
- Sunshine
- Warmth

White

The universal colour of peace and purity. Find it in logos as reversed text or negative space.

- Cleanliness
- Innocence
- Sterile
- Purity
- Refined
- Simplicity
- Surrender
- Truthfulness

Blue

A calming colour that can stir up images of authority, success and security. It can be seen extensively in government, medical and fortune 500 company logos.

- Authority
- Calm
- Confidence
- Dignity
- Established
- Serene
- Power
- Trustworthy

Red

An intense colour that can summon strong emotions from blood and warfare to love and passion. Used in logo design to grip the view's attention and has been known to raise one's blood pressure or make people hungry.

- Action
- Aggressive
- Danger
- Energy
- Excitement
- Love
- Passion
- Strength

Orange

Combining red and yellow's attributes, it's often used to draw attention. Find it used in logos to create playfulness, stimulate emotions or even appetites.

- Affordable
- Creativity
- Enthusiasm
- Fun
- Jovial
- Lighthearted
- High-Spirited
- Youthful

Green

Represents life and renewal. It is a restful and soothing colour but can also represent jealousy and inexperience. Find it in used in companies that want to portray themselves as eco-friendly.

- Crisp
- Environmental
- Fresh
- Harmony
- Health
- Healing
- Money
- Tranquility

Pink

A feminine colour that conjures feelings of innocence and delicateness. Often used in logos to add a feminine flare.

- Appreciation
- Delicate
- Femininity
- Floral
- Gentle
- Gratitude
- Romantic
- Soft

Brown

Brown indicates nature, woodiness and utility. It's in used in logos related to construction and legal logos due to its simplicity, warmth and neutrality.

- Calmness
- Depth
- Earth
- Roughness
- Richness
- Subtle
- Utility
- Woodsy

Purple

Implies royalty, mystery, spirituality and sophistication. As a combination of red and blue, it has both warm and cool properties. Find it in many education related and luxury product logos.

- Ceremony
- Expensive
- Fantasy
- Justice
- Mystery
- Nobility
- Regal
- Royalty

Grey

Neutral and cool, grey is often used for the type within logos because it's neutral and works well with most other colours.

- Authority
- Corporate
- Dullness
- Humility
- Practically
- Respect
- Somberness
- Stableness

Colour is one of the most powerful forms of non-verbal communication designers use. Colour offers an instantaneous method for conveying meaning and messages in logo design. It's important for designers to use colour appropriately and understand the meaning behind the colours they choose.

Door 5

Brand

Analyze the compition Among the keys to producing a successful brand image is to differentiate yourself from your rivalry. You will have to know how buyers see your rivalry. You have to recognize how your rivals differentiate themselves from other people. In addition to that, you ought to know your rival's fortes and failings. Your business may benefit from knowing this info by learning from their failings and learning how to distinguish your company from the rivalry. Identify your fortes Now that you recognize your rivalry's failings you are able to start to center your company's fortes. Perform a target market analysis, learn from it, and utilize it to your advantage. This is a valuable tool to confirm your company's fortes are in fact crucial to your target market. Once you've recognized your fortes, and what fortes are significant to buyers, you are able to think about ways to successfully market these to the world and involve them in your branding campaign.

Know your buyer is is key. Know your audience . Models , Actors Know your audience.

Know their buying behavior.

How frequently do they buy?

Do they purchase only during sales or promotions?

Do they purchase an array of products or services or simply a select few?

These are questions you ought to ask to better market to your buyers. In addition to that, know your buyer's lifestyles, needs, mentalities, and attitudes. Knowing and working with these personality traits are likewise key to marketing success. Branding is much more than simply a thoughtful logo or slogan and it's more than simply a unique color scheme. Make certain your company truly represents what your brand identifies you with. For instance, if one of the traits your brand identifies your company with is politeness, be polite. This means every employee from the receptionist all the way up to the CEO has to live your brand. Be An Expert Demonstrating yourself as an authority in your field will help you acquire both recognition and respect. As luck would have it, that recognition and respect transfers immediately to your company. If individuals trust that you truly recognize what you're talking about, they'll feel great about investing in your product. A website is the best place to begin. Construct a professional looking web site with sound and informative material and you'll have a source of authority information to direct buyers to. Remember that it's all right to give away some of your treasured knowledge free of charge. Provide the buyer something of value up front and they'll label you as a legitimate source to go to for whatsoever your company might offer. Article marketing is a particularly effective technique to accomplish that authority status as it gives you the power to distribute a small number of articles to a vast number of content-rich sites. The more places your name crops up, the more individuals will be exposed to your web site and product. A different way to demonstrate your expertise is through internet forums and blogs. This is a bit more casual than article composition. It allows you to remain in the first person and talk candidly with interested net surfers. The conversational tone utilized in such settings will put more potential buyers at ease. Not only will they view you as an authority, they'll likewise feel connected to you as a real human being. In addition to that, such places provide buyers the chance to ask questions and give you the opportunity to back up your product in the face of critique. Discover the correct places to gain recognition. Put yourself out there and command respect through that exposure. Spotlight your accomplishments and successes. Branding yourself as an authority is all about getting other individuals to realize something about you that you already recognize. Representation There ought to be a logical look and feel to every page of your site. You want your visitors to understand they haven't actually left your web site when they go to a different page. How People See You Icons for going back or to the next page, for printing the page or even the icons that line your menu ought to be all follow the same theme as your web site as part of your marketing endeavor. Every aspect of your site ought to be about your brand. Standing out from the rest isn't nearly as important as having other people recognize your web site. If a visitor travels to additional pages and they look different, they might believe they unexpectedly left your web site and then leave it all together. An easy concept for net market branding is your logo as an icon. You might then utilize this as buttons and every time an individual has to click, your logo makes an imprint. Obviously it will have to be much smaller than the main logo on your page or additional areas to be utilized as a menu icon, perhaps as small as 16 x 16 pixels, but the reduced image will continue your branding throughout your pages and offer a advantage to your network marketing effort. In addition, with this level of branding throughout your web site there will be no doubt in your visitor's mind where they are. You might even make it so a visitor bookmarking your web site will see the icon in his or her favorites, further imprinting the image. Remember, returning visitors frequently purchase more than first time visitors and keeping your image in their brains will aid your network marketing efforts With a bit of creative thinking, you might make it so prospective customers automatically think of you when they see your logo. This is among the simplest yet most effective branding techniques. This is one the number one mistakes people make in business as it pertains to advertising. Now lets define Branding:

Branding :

Branding is the process by which I create trust in my business.

The purpose of branding is really just to get my name out there. Www.brandyourself.com. It is the process by where I create a recognizable form for my business it's a trust factor it's a identity factor. Branding is what you want others to say about you. Branding is what you want others to think about you.

Questions?

What do you want others to think about you?

____

What do you want others to say about you?

____

What do you want others to think about you?

____

Door 6

Marketing

Marketing

Marketing is the process by which I create interest in my business.

The purpose of marketing is to get them in the door. Into my database, into my teleconference into my website into my place of business. I must first define what in here is for me. Once you define what in here is for you. Then you start working on your marketing campaign. Let me give you a quick example about branding and marketing and how it works together.

branding can make you more money. Marketing can make you more customers remember branding is what you want others to think about what others say about you in marketing is designed to get you interested. When you do a good job in marketing people get interested but without fail they will go back and they'll look for verification and validation and that is branding. Branding and marketing will always be married. If you do a good job of getting people to trust your business then your business will grow.

Branding should always cost you money.

Whereas marketing should make us money.

Marketing should always be a return on your investment. With marketing you should know exactly what your marketing budget should be. It doesn't matter if you spend five dollars or $500, but you need to know what it is going to. Once you've established your marketing budget is, then you'll be out to do some different marketing campaign you will be able to effectively target your audience.

Now my rule about marketing is very simple you can lead a horse to water but you can't make them drink it. But with good marketing you can sure make him thirsty.

We call this environmental marketing. With environmental marketing you want to position the client strategically to be thirsty for your product and services.

Remember that marketing is:

do they need your product?

Remember my pet rock people paid millions for those rocks. In the 60, 70 they sold a ton of these products kids and adults bought a Pet Rock.

What about a company called Evian that sells water. People spend millions on bottles of water as a matter of fact in fact people told me that Evian spelled backward is naïve, because marketing is not about if they need your product, it's really about do they want your product, and if you find that you're not doing a lot of sales it's because you're not making people want to buy your product. One of the Biggest lies is a quote "*if you build it they will come*". If you build it they will **ONLY** come if you market it correctly.

Door 7

Rebranding

Sometime business need a fresh start a new coat of paint. Another reason is you have combined business and need a new identity. Others are more subtle, such as outgrowing your image. If you are not clear about the business reason driving the effort, you run the risk of wasting a tremendous amount of resources. Some of the other top reasons to rebrand your professional services includes:

- You need to compete at a higher level or in a new market.

- Your brand no longer reflects who you are.

- Your business is spun off from an existing brand.

- You have a legal reason compelling you to change.

- You need to simplify and focus your message.

- You have a new marketing team.

- You are launching a new service line.

2. Research Your Target Clients

When you are clear on the business case for a rebranding, the next step is to conduct   research on your business and your clients. If you are attempting to move into a new market, that research should include your new target clients as well. The goal is to have an objective understanding of your current brand perception and competencies.

Rebranding is a door that you can use to rebrand an existing product or service. Renaming and rebranding it makes it new .

I am going to give you an example bell bottoms jeans. I was in the mall the other day and I saw these very same jeans and I said wow these are bell bottom jeans and the lady in the store corrected me and said Miss those are not bell bottom jeans those are flare cut jeans.

7 For All Mankind $198
Hudson Jeans $185
Victoria Beckham $550
Tara's Elegance Premium Jeans $103

SKINNY
OVERALLS
LADY CROPPED
RIPPED
FLARES
BOOT CUT
SUPER HIGH
THE EDITOR
THE CROPPED HIGH WAIST FLARE LEG COMBO PLATTER
CUT OFFS

rename it makes it new. I want you guys to think of new ways to rename your products and services if anyone else has called the product X then you call yours something different. I will refer to real estate the market analyst, first-time homebuyers seminars and incentives. We all do those very same things and call it the same thing we are views as the same thing in our consumers mind. We as business owner can find another creative term for the first time homebuyer program so just think of some ways you can rename your products and services.

Door 8

Repurpose

Artistic professionals, such as artists and designers, don't create from nothing. They, too, work with what's tangible and known, and they take ideas from the world around them and make them their own.

Although you may not feel as creative as an artist, you show your creativity in business when you repurpose ideas or content. It's a great way to save money, cut down on risk, and deliver value fast and consistently, yet many businesses aren't utilizing it.

Repurpose to drive solutions

Repurposing isn't a new practice, however it is a very effective tool and it can be used in any industry on any budget.

Repurpose to drive loyalty

Customer loyalty is based on value created, and no single company can truly offer widespread value on its own. Big companies have used repurposing to consistently offer value that draws customers back. I'll give you an example the number one aphrodisiac in the entire world is a small blue pill called Viagra and guess why it was created as a heart medicine but they realize it was having some interesting side effects and then based upon those side effects they repurposed it and called it Viagra.

You need to think on some ways to repurpose your products. I'll give you another examples there is an ordinary bath robe just plain white one that you get from your hotel or department store now someone got this idea of how they can repurpose a robe by turning it around to the front and called it a snuggy.

By repurpose your products and services you make them new. I want you guys to start looking at your products and services that you offer, look at what other people are calling their products and whatever there calling their product call your something different. Explore the different ways to repurpose your products and services. Here's how you repurpose your product.

What is the primary benefit of your product or service?

Let's talk about fitness we all want to be slim and we spend millions on doing so. Just go onto the internet and you will see multiple adds for fitness and weight loss. But what you really want to start talking about to get your client "in her" is to actually start talking about the clients. People know they're going to lose weight. They know they are going to feel good. You want to talk about something relevant. Let's say there is a married couple. Talk about how their husband or wife are going to regard them after they lose the weight. Let's say they are single they're looking for their mate. Talk to them on how being active helps you attract a mate. Go talk to people about the real benefits. Start talking to people about how my product will help you get healthy. But you have to ask yourself why do I want to be healthy? Real Estate people help people buy and sell houses . you can say buying a houses can help you get tax advantages. You have to ask yourself what is the benefit of the benefit? That will give you clues on how to reuse and repurpose your products and services.

Door 9

Results

If you have effectively branded and marketed your product you should see results and I am not talking about any old results. I'm talking about marketing that focuses specifically on generating clients results, marketing that focuses on generating clients let me tell you what I'm not talking about I'm not talking about marketing that caters to your ego no ego-based marketing.

Marketing is also a process. Marketing is the process by which I create interest in my business. Marketing has a purpose. Remember branding is to get my name out there. To get it out there to make sure people know about me. However the purpose of marketing is to get them in here. In into my database into my phone into my system and into my store into my place of business whatever in here represents for you. So the question for today.

Is what it does in here represent for you? And the next question.

How are you going to get them to say?

How are you going to get them to think?

I was driving around I came to a stop sign at a bus stop I looked off to my right and saw this big piece of advertising. I looked at ,and I kept looking at the sign and hit me I couldn't tell what he was selling. The main reason why I did not know what he was selling is because the biggest thing on his ad was his was his face.

In smaller print was his real estate info he was selling real estate. How was I supposed to know when the largest thing on the sign was his face? When you engage in ego-based marketing the only person who gets the benefit is you. After you define what in here is for you. You need to determine how you want them to contact you.

Do you want them to call you on the phone?

Tip: there's nothing worse than when you're calling somebody and you really wanted them to answer you got their voicemail. 80% of the people who get voicemails never leave a voicemail. People don't check voicemails they have moved away from that. people expect you to be able to answer that phone.

The purpose of marketing is to get them into the door. When they call you and they can't get in the place that you're trying to get them to because you didn't answer the phone, you hurt your brand and lose on marketing. If you are going to put your phone number on your business card this is what you need to do:

You must give your customer clear times in which you will call them hours 9 AM to 5 PM Central standard Time and that way they know they will not get you after those or before those times. They will expect to get voicemail. I also suggest only put two forms a contact on your card. A lot of people put so much contact information they can't decide on where people are to contact you. I usually recommend email address, and to your squeeze page, and if you can actually answer the phone go ahead and put that on them.

Use the voice mail to tell them the hours you will be answering calls.

Effective Business Card

With business cards you need to determine if it is a BRANDING exercise or a Marketing exercise.

If it is a **BRANDING** exercise the most important thing that's on that business card is your training and certification your licenses how long you have been in business. If it is your **MARKETING** card the most important things on your business card is your product and services that you offer.

How do you decide?

Ask yourself when you hand out your business card what do you want them to do?

Do you want to become a customer?

Or do you want their business?

If you can't decide then create two separate business cards and keep them and present what you wish during the opportunity.

<table>
<tr><td>

Regency Realty Development Group, LLC

Kasondra Spears

Broker/Owner

Office: (888) 300-9035 Ext

Direct: (512) 123-4567

Email: regencyrealtybroker@blank.com

www.spearshousehunters.com

and my real estate have too logos to be in compliance

</td></tr>
</table>

Here's another RULE:

If you put your phone number on your business card and go on vacation most likely you will not answer your phone. If in the exercise you defined in here as calling you. You must get an answering service. So that regardless of whether or not you answer it somebody will answer.

Note: BRANDING should COST you MONEY.

What things should you be spending money on?

First thing you should be spending money on, is your website. A website is key to your branding. People will determine whether your business is legitimate or not based upon your website.

<u>www.yourbrand.com</u>.A key to your website is to use WordPress HTML friendly sites NO! FLASH if your site or your marketing pages are not built in WordPress get rid of them.

Door 10

Over deliver

over delivering is a preplanned and event with an expected response.

the number one mantra of every entrepreneur is overpromise and under deliver because the fact is most people don't truly know how to overdeliver.

I am now going to teach you how to overdeliver. **Over delivering is a preplanned event with an expected response.**

Examples:

Everyone who owns a car knows that they have to go in for an oil change. They take it to a dealership. Most dealerships nowadays specialize in over delivering only the things they do when you go in now they offer you very cheap oil changes because they know you have to get the oil changed.

The preplanned event is the oil change.

Here's what they do before they give you back your car they wash your car.

Now why are they washing your car because once you get the car back you get this great feeling that hey I now have a clean sparkly car and so the preplanned event was the oil change the way that they over delivered they did something for you that you didn't know, they over delivered by giving you a car wash. This made you respond in a certain way. However, they are not done with you yet in addition to the oil change and car wash they do a free diagnostic and then they tell you Mrs. Customer we found your blank was knocking and if you don't get this thing fixed right away all the sudden your car could practically have exploded.

The preplanned event was the free diagnostic they knew they would find something wrong and you're thinking to yourself oh my God! The expected response is pure shock. You just came in for the oil change and now you have to get something fix!

This makes you nervous about going out and getting an oil change and now you're thinking to yourself however am I going to come up with the money to fix my car. The dealership has a solution to your problem

One you can get this car fixed.

You can wait till your car breaks.

Or you can finance the repairs

 You're thinking to yourself now

But then they tell you it just so happened that the part you need has to be flown in from all the way from New Zealand but say we do so happened to have it in because the person who ordered it didn't pick it up tell you what… we are going to give that to you at a 30% discount and your thinking to yourself and the expected response is great you saved me money and I feel better because my car is going to be fixed. Over delivering is a preplanned event with an expected result response.

I want to give you three guaranteed steps over to help you overdeliver in your business.

Step number one establish with the preplanned event will be.

Second step determine the client's response.

I want you guys to make a note here the clients response doesn't always have to be positive. It can be a negative response it can be a sad response it to be a happy response it to be an excited response. No matter what the response is. You will have a plan to capitalize on how your client is going to respond. When a client loses those first 2 pounds how do they feel? They're happy right even on the scale you got people on the scale that was a preplanned event she knew that the scale was going to show that they lost weight. My question to you is how would you capitalize on that? This is the time when you might want to sell them something else. Your job is not to make them feel a certain way your job is to know how they're going to feel based upon the preplanned event. Now let's say they gained weight you can respond by saying you cannot lose weight by just exercise you must diet as well and here I have some products and services that can help you out with that.

Over delivering is a preplanned event with an expected response.

Third step plan to capitalize on the client's response. Over delivering is a preplanned event with an expected response. For those people who are trying to market cheaply word-of-mouth is the cheapest form of advertising. Establish the preplanned event. Second step you have to determine the expected response. If you know how they are going to respond that you can do this third step you can plan to capitalize on it.

Door 11

Excitement

This is the excitement you generate around your product or services. No one buys from a wet blanket, if you are not excited and full of passion your clients will not be either.

Think about this every week a new movie comes out the reviewers say  BEST movie ever! The following week another set of movies come out. BEST movies ever must see and so on. You never see them say this is a great movie, or an ok movie. You have been to millions of movies some of them remakes and you know how they typically end. However, we still pay to go see movies buy the popcorn and watch the same plot line over and over again. For a movie or product to be effective you have to build the Hype! When you introduce yourself to people is their excitement? When you give your business card out are your excitement? When you stand up in a room and introduce yourself is their excitement? If you don't get excited for your business, no one else will. It's your responsibility and your duty. Now on to my Seven essential tools for business marketing:

1. You need some Internet tools.

2. Mobile phone tools.

3. Communication tools.

4. Presentation tools.

5. You need some financial tools

6. You need some organizational tools

7. You need some follow-up tools

Internet marketing tools:

You will need an email system. Email is the basic fundamental marketing tool. The purpose of an email is to provide you with some much-needed R&R relationship building and responsive

clientele. Email is a communication tool. I want you to write your emails as though you are speaking directly to that person. Do not make your emails overly formal. If you do  not know them in a formal manner the last thing the people want is to be contacted by people they do not know.

That's why if you are shopping and a store clerks ignores you, you want to leave. You step into another store they greet and are attentive you get warm and fuzzy and wallets open. Remember there some personal liberties you can take when you know a person hey so-and-so how is it going and I'm just checking in on you to see how everything was going…

reaching out to you, hey I wanted to let you know I have …. I hope you can make it. This is emailing as if I am speaking directly to the person.

Second rule of emails all email should be personalized the subject of your email should always use the person's first name why because when you  use the person's first name they are subconsciously program to instantaneously come to the state of attention. Everything after the use of your name is for you. It's the same in crowds where you think you heard your name you look around wondering who said my name? Because your program no matter what, that the moment you hear the use of your name your program to instantaneously come to the state of attention. Same thing in emails when you use people's names they come to a state of attention. You should also use their name at least two times in the body of the email. People get lots of emails and most do not get open you know why only a few people open your email? That is simple they don't think it is for them.

Example:

 If your spouse said I love you, you know it is for you. Now if they came home and said I love everyone, you would be really mad nobody wants to hear I love everybody. Everyone wants to hear I love you. Remember to personalize your emails. You do not need to put their first and last name no one goes around saying your first and last name, don't do it in emails. This'll save you a lot of time, energy, money and people will open your emails. Email open rate triple just by using their name in the body of the email. Also, be sure to thank them.

 Examples:

Hey Kasy I was just checking in. How are things going?

99% of the time they will respond back to your email.

Oh, I am doing good I am glad you reached out to me….

When writing an email asks a simple question how's your family? Here's what happens when you ask a question inside email most people don't want to be rude so they automatically respond and when they respond that creates a lane. in between you and the customer. In that lane between you and the customer, we refer to that as a relationship. Remember what I told you before the purpose of email is to build responsible clientele and effective relationship building.

First things first are how do I get them to respond? Simply ask a personal question. When you ask a simple question that you really don't care what the answer is it doesn't make any difference when they do respond. When they do respond you have created a relationship with them. A lot of people out there have big email list, and you haven't communicated with these people in a very long time. Do an experiment. Hey ______ you were just on my mind just wanted to know how have you been how is everything going? Watch how they respond. Now that you have built that door to that relationship. You now have a lane which you can drive products and services and marketing down. If you try marketing people without having a relationship that they haven't responded to yet then you have the email failure system. It is just like walking into a store and even before the person greets you… can I help you? You get shot down, No I was just looking. A great sales person will try a to build a different door to approach the client.

Hey, how are you?

I love that color of blue where did you get it?

You just build a lane or a door. You also created a relationship with the client and now they can start selling products and services. Ask simple questions it doesn't matter what the answers is.

first tool for those who want to start an email marketing **mail chimp.com, AWeber.com**.

Mail chimp it is free or low costing. When you do email automation it should not lack personalization. No one likes talking to a robot. Automation should not feel like a robot. Just think how you feel calling a call center press one for this, press two for that. It's frustrating. Automation should still feel like you. Your clients should not notice any difference between you and automation. It should be a seamless transition because you built the system.

free and paid email campaign options

Security Email System:

self-destructing emails, nonportable emails, recallable emails, nonprintable emails **www.bigstring.com**

if you have important documents. If you have confidential contracts which you are sending out. **big string.com** will allow you to send out self-destructing emails meaning that you can send somebody and email with your same email systems you don't have to change email accounts use the same email address. After they read it, it will self-destruct. You want to get someone's attention send them a self-destructing email. You can also send out sensitive data import data that you want to share with other people. You can also send out recallable emails you can send out an email that you can get back if you make a mistake you can always recall it. In addition to that you can send out emails that people cannot print. **big**

string is a must-have for all professionals that have emails that you are sending out with sensitive data in it.

E-mail assistant.

Keep your address book up-to-date **www.KWAGA.com**. In addition to what is somebody's information changes they change phone numbers this will look into every email to see if that information matches the information you have on file and if it doesn't match it will automatically update to the newest number so get that program.

Another great tool **boomerang Gmail.com** this is a very simple tool it is only for Gmail users. By the way if you don't have a Gmail account get one. Let's say you send out an email at 6 o'clock in the morning say that person does not open the email boomerang email will send him out the message again and again if he does not open the email boomerang will send the email again. This email will continue to send the email until they open the email so when you're sending out very important information make sure that somebody gets it **boomerang Gmail.com**

Everybody out there who has an AOL account get rid of it today. There are some hard-fast facts about the people have AOL accounts one they are the most targeted people for online scams because people who have AOL accounts are proven to be resistant to change, that's why they still have an AOL accounts get yourself a Gmail account it's free it's an easy to use tool and is a great tool for you to use.

top-secret tool:

readnotify.com

www.itseasyemail.com or Boombooom.com this website specializes in doing video-based emails let me tell you something video-based emails have a 300% higher open rate than traditional emails.

Now a day's people have phones and pads and tablets. Let's talk about cell phones and how they have changed. Phones use to be known for having big buttons and small screens now they are known for big screens and small buttons, because this is not a phone this is really a television screen, and

when you're looking at a television screen you expect to see moving pictures and sound. What happens when you turn on your TV and turned to CNN and instead of seeing the debate you just see a transcript you would call your cable provider and chewed them out. No one wants to see words on a screen they want to see video. Phones are mini TV's. By sending out video emails people are a lot more inclined to open that email. This system is an easy way to send out video emails you can send right from your phone you don't have to it's **easy email.com** or Boomboom.com. They have many great templates for the majority of businesses out there they have appointment reminder templates they have apologetic templates, they have templates for everything you can think of generic templates business specific templates. This system is so great that has premade videos for you so that if you don't want to prerecorded video you can use the templates that are already available to you and much more. I know some people out there still carry around a beeper or a pager.

Who has an old cell phone that is not a smart phone? I am asking you to come into the future with me. The key thing I am trying to get across here, is that there's always a better way of doing things. You will never progress until you are willing to make a fool of yourself to learn new things that is progress. You can't teach an old dog new tricks have your wonder why? One of the reasons why I believe that you can't teach a new dog old tricks is because an old dog is being vain.

Vanity

Vanity is excessive pride or admiration of one's own appearance or achievements.

Achievements

Achievements represent what you did in the past. I am talking about what you do today. My advice is to learn all the tricks you can. I want you to think like this You can teach an old dog new tricks as long as the dog is not vain. ALWAYS be coachable.

I have a question of for everybody reading this book.

What is the number one product in America?

The answer is convenience.

That's the number one product in America! It's the one product that people buy over and over again, it's the one product that never goes out of style. So, you see the question you want to ask yourself today.

Is how do you make your product convenient for your client?

The more convenient you make it. The higher likelihood they're going to

purchase it. The more convenient make it the more valuable it becomes.

Let me give you an example:

 I can go to the grocery store right now and purchase a box of macaroni

and cheese for $.89.

You can go home boil water place noodles in water let them cook down.

Then drain and add the cheese mixture and in about 20 -30 min you have

mac and cheese.

Second way

For about 175. I can add hot water and microwave mac and cheese for a

min and then place cheese powder and have mac and cheese.

Or for 2.00 I can microwave have the melted cheese already made and

squeeze it into the bowl.

I can also go over to the freezer section and get the prepackaged macaroni and cheese for $4.50.

Lastly, I can skip all of that and for 6.00 I can go to the deli section and buy it already made and hot ready to eat.

which one do you think I am going to buy?

Why is it more expensive?

Because it is convenient.

It allows them to buy and not have to think about it. It allows them to get back their time you can always make more money but you can't make more time.

So, here's a quote

"the world is getting dumber and dumber"

I can prove it. Essentially there was a time when everybody cooked. Then the microwave came along and then nobody cooked. There used to be a time when people woke up and talk to each other. Then they created the telephone, then they created the cell phone, and then they created AOL instant messenger, then MSN messenger than Yahoo messenger then they created Myspace, Facebook then they created text messaging. I saw someone have a whole conversation with LOL OMG.

Can you imagine a time where you didn't have a cell phone?

Growing up as kids we didn't have cell phones and now we cannot imagine the world without cell phone. Go be without your cell phone or internet for an hour. You cannot do it. I did it for a week no cell phone anywhere while mine was being repaired. I wanted to go buy a pre-paid one but did not. I ended up using the life proof case to fool myself I had a phone. A phone and internet are a security blanket, its connectivity. Back in the day Kids used to play with a stick and a hoop or a simple box, and now they have to have the latest and greatest technology to play with. They are no longer satisfied with the box and a stick. The world is getting dumber and dumber so you have to positioning your products and services wiser, simpler and simpler easier and easier. The number one product in America is convenience! Because it allows the clients to not have to think because the world is getting dumber and dumber. And in addition to that it allows them to get back the thing that is most valuable to them in this world **Time**.

The next time someone asks you what you are doing. Tell them you are building a door.

Bonus

Tools

What You Need

Here are the things you should acquire in your business:

1) A site that belongs to you. A Domain names. You are able to register a domain name and forward it to point at your Blog. Utilize the domain masking feature that lets your site have a professional appearance. Wwwkasyspears.com www.kasysellsaustin.com

Key Tool:

Squarespace,

Wix,

Godaddy

2) Auto Responder and Opt In box. Your visitors will most likely not make a purchase on the first try and once they leave your web site, you will not see them again. So, do get your visitors details with an auto responder opt in box and follow through with a series of e-mails. Follow up e-mails reinforces your brand name in the mind of your readers. Respectful doggedness wins sales.

Key Tool:

Mailchimp

Aweber

Infusionsoft

Constant Contact

3) Professional Email signature line. You need to have a branded email and only use this email for the business. Create tabs for saved emails example July 2018 can be a tab all emails from July go into that folder.

Casting Director summer 2018 all casting directors go there Casting directors spring, fall, winter, Property July 2018, Clients 2018. Then when you need to find an email you're not searching forever you have an idea ok I know I met them in the summer of 2018 you look into summer 2018 and blamo you have the email you can also have sub tabs in the tabs and a sub tab could be July, Aug., June 2018. The more organized you are the better. You can sub tab for each property of that month example 1234 forest lane can be a sub tab all docs go into that folder for forest lane.

Google have a 2.99 or 10. A month email service

You can be info@ yourbrand.com

Kasy@yourbrand.com

I usually do info @

Or my first name @

4) In your email you can set up a signature line and a vacation signature

line . Use a photo signature line you picture and your contact info This shows hey I am not a bot but a person. Use a professional photo of yourself. Actors and Models how professional does this sound oh you can email me a Info@kasyspears.com

Or kasy@kasyspears.com

Things you should you be investing in first thing you should be investing in SMART phones, if you don't have one get one asasp. This is because you have to know how your clients are communicating. In this new world if you don't know how they're communicating if you don't know how to communicate you put yourself at a **disadvantage.**

All your software that you should be investing in :
1. CRM and that stands for your customer relationship management system whenever you hear the term CRM automated responder system it's all just the same thing it's just a CRM a customer relationship management system all businesses have customers and

if you do you have a relationship that you need to manage effectively

. To manage those relationships, you need a system to effectively

manage those customers. By that you're gonna need a CRM.

Anything that you're doing more than three times in your business

can probably be automated. I know you're out there thinking hey

where can I get a CRM . I'm going to give you a low-cost one .

2. TOOL for CRM:

list wired.com is free.

AWeber.com

If you're working with a very limited budget go to **list wired.com** it is free it's gonna bombard you with advertisements for those working with a limited budget this is a great system. Awebber is a very costly system but is very effective and is used by many.

A big secret *"you can always make more money but you cannot make more time"* automation will help you get back more time! Take a moment and think about the things you can automate. You can send a text message to remind clients of appointments. If you had a CRM you could do just that. CRM can build landing pages. CRM can manage your website it's an all-in-one solution so get yourself a CRM today ! The goal is to give you back more of your time to invest in a CRM other things you should be investing in: If you don't have an app then you need to get one. The world is moving towards application. Anything online are now dominated by smart devices, smart phones, tablets , pads. As a business owner you have to be were the people are. The purpose of your marketing and advertising is to get results but we don't want is no ego-based marketing for those have your picture on them your business cards and all of your website. Today's a good day to stop that! You have got a think what is the product. If your product is you then that is an exception for politicians, artist then the largest thing on your advertisement should be your face. If you are not the product. Then stop and get your face off your marketing things. Here's what happens when people see faces they start to identify whether they want to do business with you or not and sometimes you're categorizing yourself without even realizing it so you have to define "in here" is to you. If you liked this book I have more books that target what you need to know in business and in life. If you would like for me to speak at your event please reach out to me via twitter @simplykasy or Youtube .

MORE BOOKS BY KASY

HOW TO BECOME A INTERNATIONAL BEST
SELLING AUTHOR

DOOR 2
CREATING OPPORTUNITIES

SOCIAL MEDIA UNICORN

REAL ESTATE INVESTING

WINNING IN REAL ESTATE

THE AGENT

DOOR 2

CREATING OPPORTUNITIES

www.ingramcontent.com/pod-product-compliance
Lightning Source LLC
Chambersburg PA
CBHW061718250726
48657CB00002B/671